Parables of Belonging

Discipleship and Commitment in Everyday Life

Lou Ruoff

Resource Publications, Inc.
San Jose, California

Editorial director: Kenneth Guentert
Managing editor: Elizabeth J. Asborno
Cover design: Terri Ysseldyke-All
Cover production: Huey Lee
Editorial assistant: Lisa Hernandez

Library of Congress Cataloging in Publication Data
Ruoff, Lou, 1946-
    Parables of belonging : discipleship and commitment in
everyday life / Lou Ruoff.
        p.   cm.
    Includes index.
    ISBN 0-89390-253-5 : $8.95
    1. Story sermons. 2. Church year sermons. 3. Catholic
Church—Sermons. 4. Bible. N.T. Gospels—Sermons.
5. Sermons, American. 6. Parables. I. Title.
    BX1756.R83P37   1993
    252'.02—dc 20   92-38844

97 96 95 94 93 | 5 4 3 2 1

Excerpts from the *New American Bible with Revised New
Testament*, Copyright © 1986 by the Confraternity of
Christian Doctrine, Washington, D.C., are used with
permission.

The epigraph (page v) by Thomas E. Boomershine is
excerpted from *Story Journey: An Invitation to the Gospel as
Storytelling,* copyright © 1988 by Thomas E. Boomershine,
and reprinted by permission of the publisher, Abingdon
Press, 201 Eighth Ave. South, Nashville, Tennessee 37202.

All profits from the sale of this book will be equally given to
Holy Trinity Church and to Holy Trinity School, Norfolk,
Virginia.

To four children:
 Nicolette & Gina Marie Pelbano and
 Carl Jr. & Marisa Fierimonte,
who are new to
 this world,
 this world of
service and
love.

Our lives are story journeys. The events of our lives connect with many other stories. But at the deepest and most profound level, the stories of our lives are empowered and given meaning by being connected with God's story...

The only way to start an exploration of the gospel as storytelling is to learn to tell stories...

But why story and storytelling? Story is a primary language of experience. Telling and listening to a story has the same structure as our experience... The episodes of our lives take place one after another just like a story. One of the ways we know each other is by telling our stories. We live in stories...

Telling a story to another person or to a group, face to face, is different from reading a book. It has its own unique dynamics. Storytelling is fun, engaging, spontaneous, and playful. To say "Let's go play." Everyone loves a good story.

Storytelling creates community. Persons who tell each other stories becomes friends. And men and women who know the same stories deeply are bound together in special ways. Furthermore, good stories get retold and form an ever-expanding storytelling network. There is something about a good story that virtually demands retelling...

Storytelling is also highly emotional. To laugh and to cry, to be deeply moved and to get so involved that you have to know how the story came out in the end—that is storytelling. You get to know other people and you get to know yourself. And the stories you remember and tell to others become the best gifts you have to give. They become yours in a special way. People become the stories they love to tell.

— Thomas E. Boomershine, *Story Journey: An Invitation to the Gospel as Storytelling,*

The word of the LORD came to me thus:

Before I formed you in the womb I knew you,
  before you were born I dedicated you,
  a prophet to the nations I appointed you.

"Ah, Lord GOD!" I said,
  I know not how to speak; I am too young.

But the LORD answered me,

Say not, "I am too young."
  To whomever I send you, you shall go;
  whatever I command you, you shall speak.

Have no fear before them
  because I am with you to deliver you, says the LORD.

Then the LORD extended his hand and
  touched my mouth, saying,

See, I place my words in your mouth!
  This day I set you over nations and over kingdoms,

To root up and to tear down,
  to destroy and to demolish,
  to build and to plant.

Jeremiah 1:4-10

Contents

Acknowledgments

Stories and parables about commitment and discipleship can never be possible without the many "ordinary" people who do for their own—and others. As a minister of the Good News, I am inspired, indeed challenged, by these "faceless" people/ministers. I become renewed and re-committed. I thank each of them.

Coming to a parish of roughly a thousand families from a community of forty families to shepherd the flock presented many unique challenges. My staff here at Holy Trinity Catholic Church in Norfolk have assisted me tremendously; their ministry speaks well for the community they serve. I thank
Julie Buhl,
Dan Owens,
Kay Fleetwood,
Kim Tougas,
Jose Caramat,
Connie Owens,
Eldon Turner,
Margrit Banta

for their love and service. I also thank former parish staff members:

> Stan Dondero,
> Sid Geiman,
> Jenny Spring,
> Tommy Thompson

and all members of Holy Trinity Parish community.

And finally, special thanks to George and Teresa Pelbano, friends in Philadelphia, for their continued love and support.

■ "The Kingdom of Heaven Is Like a Treasure Buried..."

17th Sunday of Ordinary Time (A)   Matthew 13:44-52

> "The kingdom of heaven is like
> a treasure buried in a field..."
>
> or may I say,
> "The kingdom of heaven is like
> a treasure that is re-given..."

My dad died in 1972 at the age of seventy-two. Though very reserved, he had many things to be proud of in his life. Among the top was that he was a long-distance runner.

After leaving school in the sixth grade, my dad went to work at a local firm where he was an apprentice electrician. In those days, companies, like the one that employed my dad, would sponsor marathon races so that the company's name would be more recognizable to the public eye. My dad always enjoyed running and was eager to join the company team when asked.

My dad wasn't professional enough to qualify for prize money, but he did receive unofficial prize money from people who would bet on him to win. That kind of "under-the-table" money helped my dad pay the bills and put food on the table. He did quite well for himself for a few years until America's involvement in World War I, whereupon he enlisted in the service.

After the conflict, Dad went back to work for the same company. His days of running marathons were rekindled for several more years until, in his late twenties, he called it quits.

But then the Depression brought crisis to Dad's home. Both my grandparents lost their homes and savings when the banks were forced to close. My grandparents then came to live with my parents. The family burden was very heavy, but no one really seemed to mind.

Sometime later, in the midst of financial chaos, Dad entered a major marathon race. He was thirty-one and a bit out of shape. The thing that enticed Dad was the winner-take-all prize of five hundred dollars. That was six months' wages for my dad!

Knowing it had been a few years since his last race, Dad realized he had to give this run his best. He had to get into shape; he had to win, for there was no telling how much he would get "under-the-table."

Dad won the biggest race in his life. He told me in his later years that what he made from that race alone helped his family for the better part of two years.

Money aside, what Dad cherished above all was the gold medal he received from winning "the race of his life." Dad had the medal on display in our living room for all to see and ask questions. The gold medal stayed on display in our living room for over forty years.

When Dad died, Mom passed the medal to me as a remembrance of his life and love of us. I was always to cherish it.

At the time, though, Mom was unaware that I was a reckless gambler. I wagered on anything that
> flew,
> swam,
> ran,
> jumped,
> hit,
> kicked,
> skipped, or
> moved.

In time, my luck, real or imagined, ran out. I was flat broke. It was the mid-seventies when the price of gold and silver hit sky-high. Being the addict that I was, and because the debts needed to be paid, I sold Dad's gold medal to a pawn shop for $400.

Later the same night, I told my friend what I had done. When he sternly criticized me for being a fool, I abruptly left his house.

At my priesthood ordination, in the mid-eighties, that same friend and his family traveled quite a distance to join me in celebration. Weeks later, when I was visiting my hometown, my friend and his family invited me out to dinner.

After dinner and a lot of reminiscing, my friend gave me a present to open in front of his family. Tearing the wrapping paper and bow, I opened the box and found a lost treasure: my dad's gold medal! It was truly a treasure regained!

My friend reminded me of that night ten years ago and explained that the following day he had gone to the pawn shop and retrieved my dad's medal. He had confidence in me and knew that I would overcome.

In that same way, Jesus tells all of us that the kingdom of heaven is never lost. We will overcome because Jesus wants us to enter his Kingdom.

■ Call of the Disciples

3rd Sunday of Ordinary Time (B)   *Mark 1:14-20*

It happened one weekend, a weekend that began on
Thursday and ended Saturday at dusk—after the
Passover meal. It was about
    a mission,
    a people-believing general, and
    a bunch of sorry and miserable-looking
        privates.
Looking at this rag-tag group, it was no wonder the
Jews didn't have an army, for they couldn't match
    the strength,
    the precision, and
    the discipline
of those Roman conquerors.

They simply were not suitable for making an army.

But why is he looking at me?

Now these sorry and miserable-looking privates
were about their business, were about
        fishing for food,

5

fishing for gossip.
They were shabbily dressed, ill-mannered, and their odor smothered anyone near them. These privates were loud and narrow- minded; they knew little of their or anyone's self-worth. They were part and parcel of their society, greedy and selfish. Even their forefathers' past glory—a glory praising God for their preservation and survival amid those many would-be suppressers—was forgotten and foreign to them.

But why is he looking directly at me?

This was
>the beginning of a new age,
>the beginning of humankind's greatest
>and most unusual army.

Not any army bent on possessions and land; not an army whose defense was in
>armor,
>swords,

or other weapons devised by their hands and minds; not an army that decorated one another with glossy and shimmering medals for valor, heroics, and dutiful service and conduct. It was an army whose mission was to bring the Good News in both word and deed to the inhabitants.

But why is he speaking directly to me?

Now two of these sorry-looking privates were of another man's army. They heard what this general was saying and were impressed—and they wanted *in* in his army. The general nonetheless questioned them, "What are you looking for?"

"We want to know where you come from," they responded. "We have never seen or heard of you before today." The general, not surprised, invited them to stay with him overnight. They accepted. One of them went back to his work the next morning, fishing off the Sea of Galilee, and telling his brother what an extraordinary person this general was. His excitement could not be contained. The other, more subdued and reflective, also went back to his job.

But why is he pointing directly at me?

This general came by the lake, looking for people to serve in his army. He went over to two of them who were fishing and asked them to follow him. The one who had stayed overnight with him gladly accepted, but the other questioned the general, "What good can I be for you? I'm an alcoholic." The general was pleased to hear his honesty and said to him, "Come, follow me."

But why is he reaching for my hand?

Further along the lake, the general spotted two more fishermen and approached them with the same command, "Come, follow me." One of them spoke up and said, "I have just been released from prison for various criminal charges." The general showed no sign of wanting to retract his calling. The other, however, stated his job meant child support and what would happen if he failed to secure the money. The general saw the sorrow in his eyes and said, "Come, follow me anyway."

But why is he holding my hand?

Up the road a bit, the general saw a man walking by himself and issued the same command. This particular person asked if he would be paid enough so that he would no longer be on welfare. The general said, "There will be no pay; just come, follow me."

A little while later the general saw an IRS agent at his port and ordered him to follow. The agent, recognizing the sight of a good man standing before him stood up and uttered, "Surely, you must be mistaken. I work for the government, and I have taken advantage of all sorts of people while I was making a comfortable living." The general replied, "All the more reason why I want you to come, follow me."

But why is he expecting me to go with him?

As the general went down the road with this unusual team, he spotted a man with a sword. His attire gave proof of his revolutionary hopes and aims. The general told the man to join his team. The man laughed, "You gotta be kidding! You need weapons to fight the enemy!" The general insisted, "Our revolution is the Good News of my Father." The cynical man retorted,

> "My father, and
> his father, and
> their grandfathers before,

have all been oppressed; what can you do to give us justice?"

The general ordered the man, "drop
> your sword,

your defenses,
your hatred
and come, follow me—we'll make the difference."

But why does he want me to follow him?

This general chose four other people from all walks of life and distress until he saw the youngest of all he would choose. This person, not quite seventeen, lived a life on the run. The general went to *her* and put his hand on *her* shoulder and said, "Come, follow me." The young woman replied, "Me? Me? Mine has been a life of drugs and sex,
        I have robbed and connived,
        I have manipulated
all sorts of people for money and pleasure,
I don't care 'bout anyone."

But why do you love me?

■ "And You...Who Do You Say That I Am?"

24th Sunday of Ordinary Time (B)   Mark 8:27-35

In today's gospel, at a place named Caesarea Philippi, Peter made his career. Peter made an impact for all time, for all eternity.

> It was like Notre Dame's quarterback throwing a touchdown pass with seconds left;
>
> it was like Steffi Graf winning at Wimbledon;
>
> it was like a grand slam homer winning the World Series;
>
> it was all that—and more—much more.

Jesus asked his disciples,
> "Who do people say I am?"
> "What are they saying about me?"
> "What do they feel about me?"

The disciples roared back a slew of answers:
> "They say you're Elijah."
> "Some say you're the Baptist."

"Many are saying you're a prophet."

Jesus wasn't satisfied hearing platitudes about himself. What he was actually asking was,
"Do they believe me?"
"Do they believe what I am saying?"
"Are they taking me seriously?"
"Are they doing what I am asking?"

The disciples, as if understanding what Jesus was saying, answered back:
"Yea!"
"Sure!"
"Yes, indeed!"
"Of course!"
"Why not, you're the boss!"

But Peter, not known for his intellect, was silent, still trying to make sense of what he was hearing from the Master. Peter was a bit confused, a bit concerned, for he knew that behind their backs, people thought Jesus was a bit "flaky." Peter knew people thought Jesus was
a radical,
a nuisance,
a problem, worse yet,
an embarrassment.
After all, he was thrown out of so many temples and synagogues that it wasn't funny.
He was laughed at and ridiculed all too often.
He was constantly criticized and berated by the power people.
He wasn't even accepted in his own hometown.

11

Even his own family was skeptical of
him, feeling ashamed;
and to make matters worse, the Baptist
really didn't know what to make of
him.

Then

eye met eye,
eye-to-eye
—the crossroads of life—
truth-facing-truth,
honesty-facing-honesty,
heart-facing-heart,
looking at Jesus face-to-face,
looking at God face-to-face,
looking at the mission face-to-face...

"And you, Peter, who do you say that I am?"

For one millisecond, it wasn't Peter looking at
Jesus, the mission or God—it was Peter looking at
Peter, and the gut of his insides burst with the
words: "You are the Messiah!"

"You are right, my friend," Jesus responded. "But
don't tell anyone
for they have to get it on their own;
for they themselves must find me at the
crossroads
when the chips are down,
when friends depart,
when *they* have to make a *choice.*"

Each of us has to make a choice when at the *crossroads* of life.

Not long ago a fella in his thirties came to my door. He was looking quite disheveled and depressed when I brought him into my kitchen and sat down with him. With coffee in our hands, I told him I could only spend a few minutes with him because of my other commitments. He understood.

The troubled man had a story that he wanted to share with me. He was at a turning point in his life, feeling comfortable, though fidgety, in the presence of a priest.

The man began by telling me that he had embezzled $600,000 from the corporation for which he worked some seven years ago. This company, a thousand miles from his present abode, had unsuccessfully pursued him all this time. In a sense, because of the statute of limitations, he was off scot-free.

But as he continued his story, I realized he was broke, flat busted and, to make matters worse, his wife and child had left him a year or so ago and he had no idea where they had gone. A broken man, he wanted to commit suicide. And that, I truly understood.

Taking more time with him, I offered the man my empathy and understanding; but I also offered him a challenge. "If it's happiness you're looking for, you must go back to the company and face the consequences."

He gave me all the reasons why this would be a terrifying experience for him. His own words still ring in my ears, "My humiliation would be like nothing I have ever experienced before, especially in front of my friends and co-workers."

I was certain that the fella really hadn't intended taking his life, so I restated my suggestion that he might consider going back to the company to face whatever future lay before him.

The next morning arrived. The same fella who had been shabbily dressed the day before was standing at my screen door, dressed to the hilt. A double-breasted suit with a knockout tie confronted me. Not believing my eyes, though realizing it was the same man as the day before, we sat down again with coffee. He told me he had made the decision to go back to the company and face the consequences. We bid each other good-bye and Godspeed, and I frankly never expected to hear from him again.

After a few weeks had passed, I received a letter from him. He was in a county jail awaiting his case. The man's letter was brief; he thanked me for my assistance. He wrote that he was happy.

This fella met truth at the *crossroad* of life. He met Jesus—and knew what to say. Now, *who do you say Jesus is?*

■ *Peter Decides to Follow Jesus*

21st Sunday of Ordinary Time (B)   *John 6:60-69*

And so after three days proclaiming the message
> of life,
> of real bread,
> of forgiveness, and
> of love,

Jesus departed Central Park to continue his ministry of healing, service and forgiveness. His impact
was felt; people's emotions were touched. People's
questions, for the most part, were answered. Many
left

> praising him,
> acclaiming him, and
> applauding him.

But even more left the scene dumbfounded, mysti-
fied and bewildered. Still others dispersed, criticiz-
ing Jesus and berating him.

When most of the crowd had departed, many of
Jesus' closest followers, his disciples as he called
them, also left. Jesus sensed his talk of being God's
very son and having bread/flesh of eternal life was

too much for them. Later, Jesus spotted Peter near a lake fed by the Hudson River and decided to have a talk with his buddy. Jesus sensed Peter was wavering in his faith.

Now Jesus had known Peter for a relatively short period of time, but he loved him as though he had known him all his life. Peter was the type of guy who kept everyone guessing, who kept everyone on their toes. No one knew when he would put his foot in his mouth, when he would make a colossal fool of himself. Peter was a character, a burly fellow with a hairy chest, an acre of hair on his face,

> a clumsy clown,
> a frightening brawler, and
> a lovable misfit.

Checkers was not his game; neither was tennis or golf. What he really loved was to fight and wrestle.

Jesus loved Peter immensely—so much so that they frequently found themselves in each other's company. They would go out to dinner and then to the opera together. They had a wonderful time swimming and fishing together. But more than anything else, Peter was especially fond of

> debating the prophets with Jesus,
> recalling the history of Israel with
>   Jesus;
> preaching the Torah *to* Jesus, even
> arm-wrestling with Jesus—and
>   winning!

And now Peter was stunned that
>   his friend Jesus,
>   his best friend Jesus,

would ask if he would abandon him now like some of the other disciples. Peter from the depths of his heart gave Jesus a breathtaking answer, "Jesus, to whom shall I go? All of us would be lost without you; we do believe in you.

        I believe you are God's Son, and
        I believe you are the Bread of Life."

Now that was a very bold statement for Peter to make.

Peter had
        never been known as a risk-taker,
        never been known as a leader,
        never been known to stand for his
           convictions when the going became
           rough,
but Peter had it all together at this moment.

Perhaps Peter thought he had gone too far with Jesus to simply turn back.

Perhaps he found more purpose for life than he had ever dreamed before.

Perhaps he found a profound intimacy with God while traveling with Jesus.

Perhaps he thought of all that he had given up to follow Jesus:
        relative security,
        friends,
        a comfortable living,
        a trade,
        a job,

a home,
a wife,
a culture,
a deeply-held religious tradition,
and money.

But Jesus sensed Peter was becoming increasingly uncomfortable and evasive because of the constant verbal abuse aimed at the Master, so he reiterated his initial question to Peter, "My friend, are you going to leave me?"

Now Peter had
> never been sophisticated in the art of
> problem-solving,
> never been accustomed to the art of
> choice-making, nor
> ever been superior in the art of
> decision-making—

but Peter gave Jesus a
> wholly,
> holy,

honest answer to his question: "No."

Before his response, Peter had been the most prominent disciple. With his response, Peter became their spokesperson.

■ *Why Does God Allow Pain and Hurt?*

22nd Sunday of Ordinary Time (A)   *Matthew 16:21-27*

I remember when I was thirteen years old, leaving the eighth grade on my way to high school and bragging to everyone 'cause I knew I was a big shot. But something happened to change things a bit: I was told I had to wear glasses. That popped my bubble. Now I consider myself a very ordinary-looking fella—but in those days I thought I was the worst-looking guy in the world. And having glasses besides?! I thought I was the original ugly duckling.

When the first day of school came, I took my glasses off in front of the other guys so I wouldn't look as bad as I thought and then sneaked them on when I had to see what was on the blackboard.

To make myself feel better, I thought I might as well try out for sports. I first tried
> track: too slow;
> basketball: too short;

19

football: not solid enough (my weight
was only 115 pounds);
baseball: couldn't catch;
soccer: couldn't kick straight;
tennis: wasn't coordinated.

Everyone laughed at me whenever I showed up for any of the tryouts. They would yell, "Hey you, can you run or will you fall flat on your rear?"

Those were cruel times for me, but I was determined to find a sport that I could qualify for. And I did! I always enjoyed swimming and when I tried out for the team, I impressed everyone. I excelled in everything:

the backstroke,
the breaststroke,
the butterfly stroke,
the freestyle,
relays.

I was awesome!

I made the team before all those who had laughed at me earlier. By the end of the school year, I was the talk of the campus. Some college officials came to recruit me with a tempting scholarship offer. Things were going great. But then my career came to a shrieking halt—a torn cartilage and a hernia operation! These operations allowed time to steal a lot of my natural swimming abilities. I was heartbroken and started to blame God and everyone else for my misfortune.

This experience, as unfortunate as it may have been for me, raised a vexing question: Why does God allow misfortune to wreck the lives of so many good people? Why does God let suffering bring tears to people's eyes? Why did God allow Jeremiah (and Job, among many others) to literally go through such humiliation and trial as one reads in scriptures? Why did God take away my opportunity to shine before my peers?

After reading *The Elephant Man* by Ashley Montagu, the answer became clearer for me. The story is of a man born with a miserable condition, who after experiencing one misfortune after another, is able to cope and grow and obtain "human dignity" because he experiences love, as the author testifies. Why God allows such tragedy to enter people's lives is incomprehensible, but let me try to offer an explanation.

Jesus hints in today's gospel that if you lose your life for him you will find it. What Jesus is saying is astounding to those who lack faith. The Master is saying, in effect, "whoever accepts suffering and misfortune for my sake will find a whole new life." That means not only in the hereafter, but here as well! In other words, God can use tragedy to guide people into a new and better life.

After leaving high school I worked in a small machine shop, a job I totally disliked. Another job opened up, which I took, but it didn't make me any happier. Then I heard of a bus company job that I knew would make me happy. I applied and was accepted, though I kept my old job as a security blanket.

I had to attend the bus corporation's week-long orientation program before being officially hired. Everything went well, and I learned about passes, routes, and so on. It was, however, the fourth day that shook my foundation. As part of the program, a trainee had to take a bus out of the depot with the supervisor guiding and assessing the performance. The fifth day was much like the fourth except that real passengers would be picked up.

I felt comfortable that everything would be fine until I was told I would be taking a trolley car instead of the bus I had dreamed about. The supervisor was behind me and I was quite nervous when I took the trolley out of the depot. My foot hit the fuel pedal, allowing the trolley to run out of control and hit three parked cars. The supervisor fired me on the spot! I was terribly embarrassed and humiliated. For months I blamed the Lord for allowing this to happen to me.

As I look back, it is almost impossible to believe I am who I am today. I would never have dreamed...

Have you ever thought about some of your own personal tragedies and then realized how they changed your life?

■ *You Must Deny Your Very Self*

23rd Sunday of Ordinary Time (C)   *Luke 14:25-33*

Once there was a Master whose work among the poor was heralded by everyone. The Master was recognized by all; her mission was the talk of many communities, a sort of legend in her own time.

One day a student who had ambitions of his own approached the Master. "Master," he said, "I admire you very much; I am humbled by your love of the lowly of this world. I want to be like you, I want to learn; I want to be your disciple. Is that possible, Master?" the student concluded.

The Master, eyeing the young student up and down, asked what endeavors for the poor he had to show to be worthy of discipleship.

"I have worked in the ghettos," the student quickly replied. "I have
>   taught in rundown schools;
>   cooked in soup kitchens;
>   befriended prostitutes;

influenced street gangs;
visited those in prisons;
cared for those in hospitals;
lobbied for the elderly;
assisted the retarded;
protested for peace;
argued against abortion;
pleaded for economic justice!"

"Very well," the Master happily responded. "I very much want you to come with me; I want you to be my disciple and do what I do."

The eager student asked, "What will that entail, Master?"

The Master put her hand on the student's shoulder and spoke, "My son, are you able to eat only one meal a day; and are you willing to go to bed hungry—and still be thankful?

"And when you go to bed, will you mind sleeping on the skin of a dead animal for warmth and for separating you from the freezing ground?

"Will you mind not having a bath for quite a while because there is no running water; barely enough to quench one's thirst?

"I don't know if you are aware, but there will be no paved roads, no sidewalks, no transportation. All your traveling will be done on foot—over pebbles, stones, rocks, mud, cracks, and holes.

"By the way, there's no electricity. Do you mind reading by candlelight—if we can purchase candles down the road a mile or two? There's no guarantee, my friend.

"And you know there is but one phone. If you call your family, it'll cost you $125 for the first minute.

"Perhaps, the worst part: there is no public or private toilet. If you need to go, the dusty street is the only place to use.

"Oh, do you mind terrible odors—both from animals and people? I hope not because if so you'll get sick very quickly.

"And if you do get sick, there is no hospital. The doctor comes once or twice a month, if his Jeep can get through the dangerous roads. If it's the rainy season, don't expect the doctor at all!

"A final point, my son: if it seems that I'm not paying you any attention, and you are feeling lonely and abandoned, just realize that will not be the case. The problem will be that too many people will need attention who seldom, if ever, receive any."

The student, after catching a breath or two, walked away from the Master murmuring to himself.

One's comfort is the greatest possession anyone can give up.

■ *"[I] Did Not Come to be Served but to Serve..."*

29th Sunday of Ordinary Time (B)   *Mark 10:35-45*

When the disciples followed Jesus,
>   traveling the length and breadth of
>   Palestine,
>   scanning the activities of the Teacher,

they were consumed with pride and admiration, for they realized they were in the presence of a "real live hero". The disciples had expectations of spectacular things to come because they were living in a dream world.

When Jesus arrived at the synagogue,
>   *encountering the adversary,*
>   overcoming the monumental challenges
>   of the foe,

the disciples acted as if they had won
>   the World Series,
>   the Super Bowl, and
>   the world's heavyweight title

all wrapped up in one—because they were living in a dream world.

When Jesus sent his disciples on a mission two-by-two, commissioning them the power to cast out Satan and his cohorts, instilling in them
> the gift of healing,
> the authority to forgive sins,
the disciples behaved as if they had won
> an Olympic gold medal,
> an Academy Award,
> a Nobel prize
all wrapped in one—because they were living in a dream world.

When Jesus revealed his Father to his disciples, bringing them to a unique relationship with his "Abba" ("Daddy"), and promising them everlasting life with God, the disciples saw themselves as
> "the people's choice,"
> *Time Magazine's* "Men of the Year,"
even echoed in their mind a brand-new understanding of themselves as "top priority"—because they were living in a dream world.

When two of Jesus' disciples approached the Teacher, asking for preferential treatment when he came to glory, and two others suggested to him a special place for them in the Kingdom; and when two other disciples recommended to Jesus where to place the seats in heaven—you know the usual routine...
> "Keep me in mind."
> "Hold a place for us."
> "Save a couple of chairs for us."
...the disciples seemed to be in heaven on earth—because they were living in a dream world.

But when Jesus told his disciples he was
>> an obedient Prophet,
>> an obedient Servant,
>> an obedient Son,
the disciples' dream world collapsed.

When Jesus told his disciples he was going to be arrested and advised them he was going to be degraded; when the Teacher warned his disciples he was going to die—oh, they didn't wait for him to finish—for the disciples were stunned and flabbergasted, for their dream was
>> running out of hope,
>> losing momentum.
The disciples became disillusioned—because their dream was crushed and they could no longer live in a dream world.

But when the disciples recovered, they renounced favoritism and special privileges because of the honor of their mission. The disciples knew they were to travel untested land, realizing dreams were uncommon to many people.
>> When the disciples offered hospitality
>>> and shelter to the homeless and lonely;
>> When the disciples comforted people
>>> with AIDS;
>> When the disciples sought better health
>>> services and facilities for those left
>>> ignored by society;
>> When the disciples pleaded mercy for
>>> the condemned killer;
>> When the disciples visited and assisted
>>> the many ill people and elderly;

When the disciples called for
negotiation rather than war;
When the disciples' voices clamored to
right wrongs—
they knew they were in the real world.

■ A Community Begun

Pentecost Sunday (A)   *John 20:19-23*

In the plush office of the vice-president of marketing, the executive who occupied the office was readying himself for an employee who was to be informed he would be replaced. The once-highly regarded employee entered the office at the executive's request. With a smile, the executive politely invited the employee to have a seat in a chair that barely allowed one to look across the long and elegant mahogany desk behind which the executive sat.

In a condescending manner, the executive began to lecture the employee about his conduct, which had violated long-standing company policy.

"Our enormous growth," the executive began, "depends on our continual pride in our image. This firm hired you some two thousand years ago because your image was right for us, a new concept for us all to see." Then with a scolding voice, the executive reminded the harassed employee that the firm had broken away from a three-thousand-year-old corporation because it had become mired in its own laws, lacked leadership, and failed to generate earnings that would have rejuvenated life. "That old firm," the executive explained, "was paralyzed in its own authority, ignoring demands for imaginative and profitable investments."

"Since you joined this firm," the executive lamented, "you have been
> an irritant,
> a distraction, and
> a hindrance

to our objective of securing a sound, economically based firm, able to expand and offer superior growth to our stockholders. Our financial analysts are in a quandary about your calling us to task, demanding that the firm stop investing in Third World countries unless improvements are made in human rights. You were told long ago to lay off political issues that are of no concern to this firm, but you went right ahead, damaging the company's reputation."

The employee tried to answer the charge but was quickly subdued by the vice-president. "Please, I don't need for you to respond, for I know what you'll say: that the profits from these investments serve only the small minority who are in power and have position. I totally refute that claim; anyway, it is none of your business."

The executive called attention to another area of disagreement. "You became increasingly aggravating to us when you issued a 'living wage' plea for all employees. Your plea could not have come at a more inopportune time, especially in light of our long-range fiscal planning that has yet to be completed. This plea of yours further disturbed the company because we know what's best for our employees, many of whom are

> hapless,
> hopeless, and
> pathetic.

You above all should understand that! That is why this firm came to be—that the unfortunates be directed by our centuries-old guidance. In discussing your proposal in public, you are giving people a vision for the future. We cannot tolerate that! My God, what would happen to this firm if people began to see themselves as valuable? The people would be clamoring to have a voice in this organization—and what will happen to us? No, no, don't explain yourself. It's of no use.

"Finally," the executive concluded, "I would be remiss if I did not tell you that the company finds it impossible to accept dissent within our firm. You cannot continue being a good employee and dissent at the same time. The two are incompatible. The company sees your dissent as a grave error—and because of this unacceptable behavior, the firm is dismissing you from your post, effective immediately. If you will kindly wait in the adjacent room, my secretary will see to it that you receive your severance check."

As the employee lifted himself from his seat, he issued a sober reminder to the executive, "I shed my blood once for the firm—and many times thereafter. I will shed my blood again for this firm, and all firms, and all peoples despite your attempts to dismiss me."

The unaffected executive responded, "The firm's decision is unequivocal; I have a dozen or so people to interview for your position, so please wait in the adjacent room."

The interviewing process began. The executive entered the lobby, where a number of applicants were waiting for their interview with the vice-president.

The executive called for "Mr. James Alphaeus." The candidate entered the vice-president's office and was peppered with an assortment of questions. Midway through the lively exchange, a hitch developed that all but eliminated the candidate from consideration. Sensing the candidate was too skeptical and too assertive, the executive told the candidate to await word about his employment and directed him to the waiting room, the same room where the dismissed employee was still waiting for his severance check.

James Zebedee was the next candidate called from the lobby by the executive. The interview ended rather suddenly when the executive felt that the candidate was "a snob and a know-it-all." As with the first candidate, the vice-president sent the candidate to have a seat in the waiting room.

It did not take the executive long to conclude that his next aspirant, Matthew Levi, was not trustworthy. "A con-artist, a hustler," the executive thought while showing Matthew to the door.

His hope ran high as the executive called Mary Magdalene to his office. He greeted Mary, saying, "I read in your application that you are from Nazareth. Where is Nazareth?" But even during this interview, a discomfort developed in the mind of the executive. Mary was precluded from further consideration because of her flawed reputation. She too was shown to the waiting room.

The list of acceptable candidates dwindled until finally the last candidate entered the office of the vice-president. "Ha! Peter Simon, have a seat," the executive said enthusiastically, suspecting Peter to be his man at last. But as the interview progressed, the vice-president found Peter Simon to be

> arrogant,
> a loudmouth, and
> a buffoon.

The executive, as with all the others, escorted Peter to the waiting room. As the executive peered into the room, he heard a lively exchange and interaction between the dismissed employee and those seeking the vacant position. The vice-president returned to his office and tried to assess which candidate was the least offensive to hire. Finally, with his mind made up, the executive went to the waiting room again to announce his choice.

As the executive opened the door, he found the room *empty...*

Though Jesus chose people with flaws and faults, our Church has been around for some two thousand years. It can be stated that the Church is made up of Saints and Sinners but that we follow the Mission of the Church as best we can. Renowned for his theology and perceptions, Rev. Walter J. Burghardt, S.J., gave his insight into the Church that he loves and serves while giving his commencement address at St. Mary's Seminary and University in Baltimore in 1970:

> In the course of a half century I have seen more Christian corruption than you have read of. I have tasted it.
>
> I have been reasonably corrupt myself. And yet I love this Church, this living, pulsing, sinning people of God with a crucifying passion. Why?
>
> For all the Christian hate, I experience here a community of love.
>
> For all the institutional idiocy, I find here a tradition of reason.
>
> For all the individual repressions, I breathe here an air of freedom.
>
> For all the fear of sex, I discover here the redemption of my body.
>
> In an age so inhuman, I touch here tears of compassion.
>
> In a world so grim and humorless, I share here rich joy and earthly laughter.
>
> In the midst of death, I hear here an incomparable stress on life.
>
> For all the apparent absence of God, I sense here the real presence of Christ.

■ *Repent! Reform!*

2nd Sunday of Advent (C)   *Luke 3:1-6*

John's voice in the wilderness
> still reverberates here in today's gospel;
> still reverberates in our world; and
>> hopefully,
> still reverberates in our homes.

Two thousand years later we hear the same spirit of
John—though in the voices of other people—saying,
> "Reform!"
> "Repent!"
> "Salvation is yours!"
> "The Messiah is coming!"

> Sometimes,
> many times
we treat those voices as if the words were still coming from the wilderness—as if to say,
> some other planet,
> some other reality,
> some "Twilight Zone."

John the Baptist was preparing the way for Jesus to come and visit our world, for God to live with us. John says first we have to repent and reform, then salvation and forgiveness will be ours for all eternity.

Our world is
        changing,
        re-forming.
No longer are the likes of
        Stalin,
        Khrushchev,
        Brezhnev
the movers and shakers of the world. But have we replaced the dictators of our world and become the dictators of our own community, of our neighborhood, even of our own homes? If so,
        Reform!
        Repent!

But
        there's no hurry;
        there's plenty of time;
        no need to rush;
        there'll be other Advents;
        Jesus will come again, at another time.
        John will always be somewhere out
          there in the wilderness, some
          "never-never land."
        So, what's your hurry?
        Take your time;
        there's plenty of time left.

Communism is much less a menace in our world today than a decade or two ago—but is having other gods better than having *no* God? Are our gods

>money,
>prestige,
>power,
>sex,
>self?

If so,

>*Reform!*
>*Repent!*

But

>there's no hurry.
>There's plenty of time left;
>no need to rush.
>There'll be other Advents;
>Jesus will come another time.
>He'll come again—he always does.
>So, don't get panicky;
>you know good old John will be back to
>>do his thing from the wilderness every
>>year—
>so wait till next year!

Today, the nuclear threat, though still a peril to our world, causes less tension than a decade or so ago. It seems our world is *re-forming* itself. Are we? Or has violence permeated our homes? Have

>alcohol abuse,
>drug abuse,
>child abuse,
>parent abuse

and all the other abuses we humans have the capacity to inflict on ourselves and on one another, be it physical or mental, ruined our family life? If so,

> *Reform!*
> *Repent!*
> The Messiah is coming!
> Joy is about to come into our world, into our homes.

But

> what's the hurry?
> There's plenty of time!
> Don't get too concerned!
> There's no need to rush.
> You know death always claims the other guy.
> So, I wouldn't get too upset.
> Plenty of time left.
> Putting it off another year won't hurt; there'll be more Advents.
> And you can bet your life that John will be preaching reform and repentance for another two thousand years.
> So, what's all the fuss?
> Don't bother this year.
> Plenty of time left!

Many great strides have been made in the last two decades to save our environment. We are more conscious about air pollution, hazardous waste, wildlife, acid rain, energy, water. In fact, we're concerned about all of God's creation—but are we just as concerned about the pollution of

> our dislikes,
> our hates,

our wants,
our greeds?
Do we ignore the harm that these cause other people? If so,

Reform!
Repent!
The Messiah is coming!
Peace is about to come to us all!

But

don't get upset, please, thinking you
have to go off marching away to
straighten up.
Relax!
Wait,
there's more than enough time left;
don't give it another thought;
there's no need to rush.
Remember, death comes to the other
guy—not you.
You'll have plenty of time to change;
there'll be other Advents!
If you miss this time,
you'll catch him next year, like
the bus,
the train, and
the plane that always come again.
So, don't rush.
Repent,
reform
some other time!

Generosity is more apparent in our world now than I have ever experienced. Assistance is given to the people

of Chernobyl,
of Mexico,
of Africa,
of India,
of The Philippines,
of Iran,
of Poland,
of San Francisco
or wherever tragedy and disaster strikes.

This outpouring of love is sometimes overlooked—
but don't ignore the love given to us:
love of community,
of family,
of *life*, and the
love of God
who came to live with us—and resides within us. If,
in fact we have ignored these loves, then perhaps
this is the time to
Reform!
Repent!
And hurry!

■ *Blessed Are the Peacemakers*

Once upon a time in a town not too far from here there lived a nine-year-old boy. The youngster's name was Alfred, Alfred Smith, though he wanted to be called by his nickname, "Al". Everyone called him Al except his parents. They liked the name Alfred, especially his mom, who had named him after her father, whom Alfred had never met.

Alfred would always tell his parents he would like to be called Al because it was easier to say, to spell, and to remember. And besides, Alfred was a silly name. Whenever there was a dispute in Alfred's house, it was always brought up at the dinner table, and after some discussion an agreement was settled upon. And so it was with the name Alfred.

That was the way the Smith family settled most disputes involving Alfred. Like the time Alfred wanted to punch one of the neighborhood bullies for wrecking his bike. Another time, it was the language Alfred was using when he was around his friends. Nothing was too sacred to be discussed at the dinner table. Even the topic of why Alfred didn't have a baby brother or sister. Everything was honestly talked about.

Another thing the family did at the dinner table was to read a scripture passage before eating. Alfred always liked the stories he heard, but he especially liked the part about the "peacemaker." Alfred felt he could always be a peacemaker—and do it well.

Then something began to happen in Alfred's house.

Things stopped being discussed at the dinner table. In fact, there were now very few dinners at home. Alfred could only guess at what was happening. He heard Mom and Dad yell at one another. Things like:

"You're lazy!"
"Mind your own business!"
"You're drinkin' again!"
"Get off my back!"
"Where's the paycheck?"
"Don't talk to me like that!"

All Alfred knew for sure was that Mom was working two jobs and was seldom home, while Dad was home a lot but acting angry. This made Alfred uncomfortable and upset.

Alfred tried hard to be a peacemaker—but what do you do when Mom and Dad don't want to talk to each other anymore, except to argue and fight? Alfred became sad and began to hide in his room.

After some time, Mom and Alfred left the house they were living in and moved into an apartment. It was called "separation and divorce."

Things were rough for Alfred; so was the neighborhood—these bullies were rougher.

As time went on, Alfred started blaming himself for what had happened. He really didn't know what he had done, but he felt he must have done something. "If only I could have said...," Alfred kept saying to himself. What was really disturbing was the fact that Alfred loved both his parents very much and wished he'd been a better "peacemaker."

Because of all the confusion, Alfred started blaming himself for *everything* that went wrong. In school, Alfred's grades tumbled, and he called himself stupid and began to dislike himself. Whenever Alfred did this, he would go out in the sunlight and hide in his shadow. This was a way for Alfred to seek comfort, for in the darkness of the shadow he didn't have to deal with reality. Alfred would just let reality go away.

Alfred, the star basketball player for his school, began to miss practices, and in the biggest game of the season, he blew passes and easy lay-ups, which disappointed his teammates. Alfred blamed himself and called himself dumb. The next day, he stepped into his shadow again. This time the shadow was bigger because Alfred felt he was a bigger jerk; nonetheless, Alfred found comfort hiding in his shadow or "mask," as he called it.

Alfred's best friend began to see an abusive side of Alfred. They began to fight like cats and dogs until Teddy stopped coming around. This separation made Alfred all the more content to blame himself. Alfred called himself such names like "no-good" and "worthless." Again, to get away from the things that would be hurting him, Alfred went to the sunlight to find his shadow and hide there. And by this time, the shadow had grown almost as tall as he was— that made Alfred feel just great!

Finally even Alfred's relationship with his mom and dad became so tense that nothing seemed to work except hiding in his shadow. But now Alfred's shadow began to overwhelm him and frighten him.

Though he tried to escape, Alfred couldn't. Alfred finally realized that hiding in his shadow was no substitute for true family experiences and friendship, no matter how imperfect they seemed to be.

Alfred tried to escape his shadow again and again, but to no avail. His own shadow was preventing Alfred from leaving. Alfred screamed and hollered but the shadow was determined not to let him go. Alfred felt doomed; he felt his entire life would have to be lived in his own shadow.

As Alfred was crying, he heard the voices of his friends and parents. They were expressing in their own way that he wasn't the problem—he wasn't to blame.

Alfred's mom spoke of her need for his joy...

Alfred's best friend expressed his need
for his loyalty...
Alfred's team expressed their need for
his talent and spirit...
Alfred's school expressed its need for his
life...
Alfred's dad expressed his need for his
love.

Alfred listened.
Alfred began to leave his shadow.

Each step away from his shadow brought Alfred to
a better understanding of himself as a "peacemaker." All he needed to do was to be present to
others.

■ "What Profit [Is It] to Gain the Whole World...?"

22nd Sunday of Ordinary Time (A)   *Matthew 16:21-27*

There was once a prince who wanted to be king. The prince loved the admiring people who gathered whenever his father, the king, traveled the country; he so wanted the attention. Though the prince was received kindly wherever he went, it wasn't as if he were king.

As fate would have it, one windy day the king lay critically ill in his chamber and the prince was summoned to his father's bedside. To the surprise of everyone, particularly the prince himself, the pragmatic king relinquished his throne to the prince with an urgent plea: "Always listen to the wind, my son. The wind will be your friend, if you allow." The dying monarch's voice perked a bit as he continued, "The wind is mightier than any army, swifter than twenty thousand horses, and one hundred thousand angels cannot match its kindness. Never waiver from its advice."

47

Nodding he head in acknowledgment, the prince saw his father draw his last breath.

On a breezy coronation day, from the castle's brightly colored balcony, the new king heard the throng of people shouting for the first time,
> "Hail!
> Hail!
> Bravo!
> Hooray!
to our new king! May you always have health! May you live a hundred years!"

Regarding well the spectacle of endless seas of eager hands and excited admiring crowds, the debonair king traveled the length and breadth of his kingdom, seeking the people's adulation,
> "Hail!
> Bravo!
> Hooray!"

What was disconcerting to the king, however, was that his kingdom was small, too very small. "If only my kingdom were larger," the monarch contemplated, "the adulation of my people would be more pleasing to my ears."

"This cannot be accomplished," the king further thought, "unless I bring the best minds into my court." To acquire the much-needed land that would ensure the world's largest empire, the monarch selected the most decorated general in the country. In no time, a mighty army, the likes of which the land had never seen, was formed and subsequently waged war on friend and foe alike.

The great army conquered enormous territories, which extended the kingdom far beyond anyone's imagination. When peace was restored, the masses saluted the king and his entire entourage with all the enthusiasm a victorious empire could offer.

"Hail!

Bravo!

Hooray

to our illustrious sovereign! May you live a hundred lifetimes!" his subjects shouted over and over.

In the meantime, a slight wind began blowing, rustling the fallen leaves, trying to divert the king's attention. But the wind was virtually eclipsed by the protracted clamor of the crowd. The king never noticed. And as the wind settled down, storm clouds were seen in the distant horizon.

Peace was short-lived.

A neighboring empire, one equally as large and powerful, invaded the king's territory, causing turmoil, destruction and death. The invading army brought the kingdom to its knees. Concessions were made; half of the empire was annexed to save further bloodshed and grief. The defeat was all the more humiliating when it was learned that the king himself suffered a wound in battle.

When the hostile forces retreated to their own land, a moody, somber presence overtook the castle and the people in it, the king among them. Worst yet, a plague of discontentment and disillusionment seemed to overshadow the king's now-reduced empire. The once-buoyant people were mired in a sea of melancholy caused by the terror of a foe not far away.

The once-mighty empire seemed on the verge of total collapse, on the brink of total despair. No longer was the king hearing adulation; instead the people cursed,
> "Damn you!
> Damn you!
> Fool!"

The gloom and pessimism lingered several years in the king's land until news of the death of the neighboring monarch reached the castle. Optimism reappeared when the new monarch of the neighboring land expressed a desire for a change of climate between the two empires.

Both rulers quickly negotiated terms for the return of the king's land. When the treaty was announced, joy filled the empire. The gusting and blowing wind seemed to hover over the entire empire. Again, the king didn't notice.

So that dismay might never again see the light of day, the king issued a proclamation: May joy forevermore rule in the kingdom! Making sure his proclamation would be carried out, the monarch hired the most proficient musician in the land.

Singers of all types were welcomed. Lyrics and melodies of all sorts were invited; humming and whistling were wholeheartedly encouraged. Bands of every variety, instruments of every description, marchers with drums and fancy costumes rallied the entire population out of the doldrums into a new period of happiness.

Total happiness was once again in evidence everywhere the now-liberated king traveled.
"Hail!
Bravo!
Hooray!"
the faithful cried with new fervor. The king lavished in this new-found adulation, while the wind's stiff breeze caused havoc with robe and flaps. It was as if the wind had a message to deliver to the king but, as before, no impression was made upon the monarch. The wind's message lay dormant.

One cool windy day, however, the king fell ill from the wound he had suffered in battle. His body was limp and paralyzed. The call went forth for the best physician.

Doctors from every part of the kingdom came, advised, prescribed. The best medical minds were at a standstill as to what could be done. The simple fact was: nothing could be done to relieve the king.

In due time, the king's illness was so debilitating that his brother became the reigning monarch.

The former king could only remember how it used to be when the good wind was blowing.

"What profit would there be for one to gain the whole world and forfeit [one's] life...?"
(Matthew 16:26)

■ *"...You Will Deny Me..."*

This glimpse into Jesus' final meal tells us much about his love and the love of his Father.

Because of
> all that Jesus stood for,
> all that he was doing,
> all the self-confidence that expressed
> itself,

the conspiracy to kill him was already underway, indeed rapidly unfolding, unraveling even as he and his disciples were eating supper with each other.

Indignant as ever, Peter all but dismissed the charge and insight Jesus had about his beloved disciple's fidelity to him. Solemnly he told his friend that before it was over, he, Peter, would deny any knowledge of him, his Master.

The trust that night must have been incomprehensible. The trust that Jesus had in Peter despite the unfolding events; the trust that Jesus had in his

Father that "...not as I will...[but]...your will be done!"; the trust God had in the man and his mission and ultimately in us—tells us of an unending bond our Creator has for the world and its inhabitants.

Jesus knew humanity's fault, his disciples' weakness, and society's tendency for doing evil. Yet for all its imperfections, Jesus never abandoned humanity but still empowered his disciples to carry on his mission so as to reveal his Father's great love.

I guess it all comes down to a basic point. It is something
>we all have in common, that
>we all share with one another:

>We're imperfect creatures.
>Our planet is imperfect.
>Evil pervades
>>our existence,
>>our history, and unfortunately, even
>>our future.

I suppose, if we were given a foretaste of what to expect of the world we were going to be living in and of our human tendency, and if we were given the option of whether to enter it or not, we would all say something like, "Thanks, but no thanks." Because of all the imperfections, the weaknesses, the evils, the faults, the sins, life is truly a scary enterprise to be involved in—and yet we are. And like Jesus, who didn't abandon Peter at his most sinful time—neither will he abandon any of us.

Back when I was fifteen, bugging the heck out of my father to teach me how to drive so that I could be like all the other guys with their "wheels," my dad tried to give me some words of wisdom about the hazards of the road I was about to embark on. Though I needed him, I rejected many of his appeals and suggestions.

The big day came when I received my learner's permit, though it was six months before I turned sixteen. My dad, though ever cautious, agreed to teach me to drive—his way. What that entailed was getting up at 2 a.m. and going to the local supermarket lot and getting the feel of the car, the road, the turns, parking, backing up, and stopping and going.

After a few times driving on the empty market lot, I thirsted for the big road, to be out there with all the others. I suppose I couldn't wait to grow up and be one of the bigger people. My dad had other ideas: he wanted to take me on the side streets at 2 a.m. so I could get the feel of an ordinary city street and adjust myself to parked cars. He felt that time of the morning, with few moving automobiles and pedestrians, would make all of us comfortable. I rudely complied for a few days.

The time had come when I felt it was truly my turn to take to the road and show them all. But again, my dad had other ideas. Dad wanted me to drive on the side streets during regular traffic time before going out on the highway. It made some sense to me, but I felt I didn't need any more preliminaries. Again, I was rude to my dad. I insisted going out on the highway.

Roosevelt Boulevard is one of the busiest highways in Philadelphia—and it was right in front of my house. Being able to drive on that road would make me the biggest of all bigshots! So, reluctantly my dad allowed me to go on Roosevelt Boulevard and test the road—all sixteen lanes! At midday, as confident as ever, I took to the road with my dad next to me—and I was going to show everyone, Dad included.

Once on the boulevard, three lanes into the traffic, cars whizzing past me at sixty and seventy m.p.h., I began to get scared, began to panic. I suddenly realized that this boulevard was too big for me. Suddenly this bigshot became a smallshot. I kept looking over to my dad for assistance, but he couldn't do anything for me until I got to the side of the road. I began to cry—some bigshot! But Dad was there to calm me down, talked to me as I eased myself and the car to the roadside. Dad guided me through it all—but he never made me feel that I was a smallshot. And that's the reason I'll always love my dad.

God is like that. We all feel we can do things without God; although God knows better, the Lord allows us to make our own mistakes, commit our own sins, assert our own denials—yet when things get out of hand and we feel like we're truly smallshots, God is there to guide us to reconciliation—certainly with ourselves (as with others). God, like my dad, will not allow our faults to stand between the love and forgiveness that is forever offered. The road that we are all on is big and dangerous, with many

potholes that will test our relationship with God.
Falter though we will, God's presence will always
be there. As with

> Peter's arrogance,
> my rudeness,
> our sinfulness,

God will never abandon us.

■ *Mission of the Disciples*

Jesus sent his disciples out on a mission of hope and love; he gave them their final instructions:

Leave your suitcases behind:

Where you are going you won't need a change of clothing too often. Whatever little clothing you are wearing, washing them daily will put you in touch with my people. Your Pierre Cardin wardrobe won't be necessary where you are going—and anyway, it's not in vogue anymore!

Leave your car keys behind:

Where you are going there's no Sears & Roebuck store, no Pizza Hut, and no James Bond movie playing anywhere. There's not even a Burger King or a McDonald's anywhere in sight. Where you are going, there are a lot of empty bellies that need to be fed and cared for. Oh, by the way, don't expect to see any modern hospital franchises—"HumanCare" only means human care to my people simply because they have little, if any, monetary means. Incidentally, your medical insurance will not cover anyone—not even you!

Leave your wallets behind:

Where you are going, money buys only guns and bullets, tanks and machine guns, jets and bombs, ships and missiles. And no, MasterCard and Visa are not recognized where you are going—perhaps in a hundred years or two. Where you are going, illiteracy is spreading—and you thought it was a problem long since conquered. Speaking about communicating, Ma Bell is not too organized where you are going—so don't expect too many long distance phone calls. Practically speaking: don't expect any calls. Before I forget, mail is delivered where you are going—but it does take a while!

Leave your rings and other jewelry
behind:

Where you are going, there is an abundant supply of earth's natural resources, but greedy profiteers are making sure they are shipped to other parts of the world so that other people's lifestyles can be more fashionable. Where you are going, competition, manipulation and deception are rampant and chaotic. Where you are going, you must be a slave for one another, never one above the other.

Leave any weapons behind:

Where you are going, violence and disorder will be commonplace; where you are going, political and religious freedoms are suppressed; where you are going, civil liberty is unknown; where you are going, human rights are unspeakable—but you must always have peace on your lips and in your hearts. Where you are going, illwill may very well distract you from your mission, but know that I faced this too—and I will be with you.

At the end of Jesus' instructions, some of the disciples began murmuring to each other, "Where is he sending us to, Timbuktu?" Others began to speak up, saying they were hoping to go

> to Honolulu,
> to Monte Carlo,
> to the French Riviera, or even
> to the Swiss Alps!

Jesus replied, "The Kingdom of God must be joyfully experienced in all parts of the globe, every nook and cranny. Wherever people are, there the Kingdom must be experienced."

One of the disciples approached Jesus, "You have painted a bleak picture for our journey. What are the essentials we need to call forth the Kingdom of God?"

Jesus answered,

> "Bring yourselves,
> bring your hearts, and
> bring the joy of understanding God
> more than ever by being witnesses to
> my love.

Jesus continued,

"The people you travel with are more
important than the things in your
suitcases.
The people you visit are more important
than the cars you left behind.
The people you touch are more
important than all the money in all
the wallets of the world.
So bring
yourselves and
your hearts,
and communicate that love of God that I have
shown for you to
everyone,
everyone in all the continents of the
world."
You have the power to make lives brighter because
you have seen the Son!

■ *"Love One Another..."*

6th Sunday of Easter (B)   *Mark 1:40-45*

> "...love one another as I love you...
> It was not you who chose me,
> but I who chose you..."

There are times when I question God. That is to
say, I question God's love for me. To be even more
blunt:

> I know me; at times,
> I don't like me 'cause
> I know I can be
>   a real jerk,
>   a real pain in the neck.

Yet I know God loves me—I just ask "Why?" Would
you continue to love someone who makes shambles
of oneself and others? But our God does...and I ask
why.

Perhaps a story about my Aunt Kate and Uncle Cy
might shed some light on the question.

When I was twelve, I met my Aunt Kate for the
first time. She had recently married my Uncle Cy.

No one, not even my aunt's brother, my dad, thought it would ever work out.

My aunt was friendly, full of smiles, that first time we met. I knew, however, she was the kind of person who would let no one push her around. I instinctively knew she wasn't anyone's fool; she could handle herself.

Aunt Kate sold hosiery and similar merchandise at the Port of Philadelphia, where the merchant ships would come to dock. My aunt would sell her wares to the men onboard for their wives and families overseas. She was full of confidence and had all the "street knowledge" about selling. She had an uncanny ability to speak her mind. She could, and would, often embarrass many of the longshoremen with whom she came in contact. But they loved her. After all, she'd been coming to the pier ever since she was fifteen, at the height of the Great Depression. My aunt's business could rival any of her competitors.

My dad, rarely an outgoing person, truly loved his sister despite all her antics. My dad just couldn't understand her ways. Many times, Dad felt embarrassed that my aunt was related to him. Whenever there were rumors about my aunt, Dad would not acknowledge any of them. Take the time back in the mid-fifties when my dad had to bail my aunt out of the city jail.

Being known as the toughest one around the port, my aunt lived up to the billing. On this particular day, she had an encounter with another person selling similar merchandise aboard the same ship. A disagreement occurred, which led to a full-scale fight, resulting in the man being thrown bodily overboard. Not only did my aunt throw him off the ship, but all his wares as well! She threw his partner overboard too! When the police arrived, the scene was hysterical: two men with all their wares in the water, crying for safety nets while legions of longshoremen applauded the heroics of my aunt in re-establishing the boundaries every pier should respect.

Given my aunt's reputation, she wasn't any kinder to the police when they questioned her, and this led to her arrest. By the way, my aunt was *sixty-five years old* when all this transpired.

You can understand now why a man like my dad, who had lived his entire life by the letter of the law, was so humiliated when he received that phone call to bail my aunt out of jail.

In her defense, my aunt was always a perfect lady around me. I always felt comfortable around her because I knew what she was like, though she didn't know I knew the stories that circulated around the neighborhood about her.

One day, however, my aunt slipped. We were in one of the best department stores in town, doing a little Christmas shopping, when I wandered off. After spending some time trying to find her, I saw some women fighting over a coat sale. Lo and behold, there was my aunt beating the dickens out of another woman. As I stood there gulping for something to say, she spotted me. Quitting the ruckus, my aunt came over to me, whereupon we resumed our shopping as if nothing had happened.

I realized my aunt was terribly embarrassed about the incident, so I never let her know how uncomfortable I had been, for fear that it would hurt her even more.

This brings me to my Uncle Cy.

My uncle was a frustrated showman. He had played in vaudeville shows in his earlier years with very little success. He looked like Ed Sullivan of television fame. He wasn't an attractive man; if the truth be known, he was homely.

My uncle was married three times; they all ended in dismal failures. Thank God, in all these marriages there were no children.

Anything my uncle ever tried ended in failure, which is why he had a severe drinking problem. In those days, one's drinking problem was seldom discussed.

Both my Aunt Kate and Uncle Cy had their good qualities as well. They were
> generous,
> sincere, and
> loving.

But one's flaws always seem to take center stage.

When my aunt and uncle met, they were in their late sixties. After a couple of years of dating, I remember my aunt telling my dad she was going to marry Cy. Dad was beside himself with shock. Not only my dad, but no one else could believe it either. It made every eyebrow in the neighborhood rise.

All my aunt's friends pointed out all my uncle's faults and failures to her; and all his friends, hers. For example:

"She'll humiliate you!"

"You want to marry someone who looks like that?"

Over all the objections, they were married.

Their marriage lasted some eighteen years. At eighty-one, when my uncle was dying, it was my aunt who nursed him to the end. My aunt's love was a long way from the rough and tumble days of the piers and docks.

Sometime later, I asked my aunt why she married my uncle. "I liked being with him," she responded. When I asked her about my uncle's not-so-good looks, she answered, saying that she never really noticed what he looked like. All she knew, she said, was that he was a good person—and a good person for her. She laughed, saying that maybe she should have noticed, but quickly added, "Nope!"

Likewise with God. God doesn't dwell on our faults. God sees inside to our heart of hearts.

■ *Hand to the Plow*

13th Sunday of Ordinary Time (C)   *Luke 9:51-62*

> "No one who sets a hand to the plow
> and looks to what was left behind
> is fit for the kingdom of God" (Luke 9:62).

I think that is an impossible task you are asking, Jesus.

I often wonder how realistic it is for people to put their hands to the plow and not to allow themselves a look back? It is a very real and extremely difficult temptation for me.

I've always been an inquisitive person, wanting to know all that is going on
>   around me,
>   beside me,
>   behind me,
often forfeiting what lay in front of me and thereby costing me the mission I was undertaking.

When I do look back, I find out many times my efforts weren't worth the time and bother it took.

That is what I suspect Jesus is telling us in this particular parable.

More fundamentally, Jesus is pointing out to us the need to be faithful to his mission, which will require steadfastness and straightforwardness, even in troubled and ambiguous times.

Like Diogenes with his lantern, I, with pad and pencil, sought to find able-bodied people who had taken on themselves a mission and never allowed themselves to look back. Being a cynical person, I knew I would not find a single person like that.

After several months seeking, I just could not find anyone who, by their own estimation, didn't take hand off the plow once the mission began. Unlike Diogenes, I found honest people who spoke of their shortcomings, be it vacillation, impatience, or plain fatigue. All my research confirmed what I already suspected: Jesus' expectation of our putting our hands to the plow without looking back is one that we cannot meet, especially in these uncertain times.

No sooner did I mouth the words, "Ha, there you go, Jesus. I told you it was an
> impractical,
> improbable,
> impossible expectation,"
when I met a young couple who told me differently. They did, the couple said, put hand to the plow and chose not to look back,
> not even once,
> not even for a peek.

This able-bodied couple, in their mid-twenties, left the high-powered, rat-race jungle of New York City and Wall Street, looking for tranquillity and peace far away in the countryside. The couple felt the environment in which they existed: the haughtiness, the greed, the smog were polluting the lives and well-being of themselves and their children. After family discussions for five years or more, a decision was made: they would move away from commercialism, from materialism, from the rat-race to the natural beauty of the countryside. It was a difficult decision to make—leaving family, friends, security—but they knew there was a better way to live happily. And they put a hand to the plow and never looked back.

Barely had I taken a breather from learning about this unexpected accomplishment when another able-bodied couple revealed they also set out on a mission and did not allow their determination to be undermined.

This Czechoslovakian couple had escaped their homeland a few years after the Russian-backed invasion of 1968.

The couple's dream was freedom, freedom for themselves and their children. Leaving their homeland was the only way to gain that freedom.

Foregoing their homeland was not without its courage and dangers, always knowing an eye might be upon them and assuming, suspecting their families they had left behind would be harassed. But freedom doubtlessly was the couple's dream; their minds set, they could not afford to look back.

Years later, having abandoned their former occupations of doctor and professor, the couple had to begin again from scratch. They eventually succeeded, succeeded by overcoming barriers and customs, and today they continue their mission of service—in freedom.

I paused to take another breather when an elderly couple, whom I had bypassed for the longest time, informed me they had put hand to the plow for fifty years or more. Before the couple had a chance to finish, I mistakenly and patronizingly congratulated them on their golden anniversary, commenting that that was an accomplishment to be proud of.

"But how did you survive married life for half a century without looking back to see what might have been," I added. Together the couple responded, "No, no."

"I don't understand," I replied.

The slenderly built, slightly hunched woman spoke, "We retired from our jobs some twenty years ago; we even left our church community where we had been so active. We decided to put all that behind us so to live in the quietness of the hills and mountains and to enjoy each other for the first time in our lives."

"But that was not to be the case," she added smiling. "My husband built our own home out of wood and logs with nails and hammer—and since we arrived he hasn't stopped helping people in the area. As for myself, I've been the busiest I've been in years, mothering a lot of young hearts."

The elderly lady must have seen the wonderment in my eyes and ended our encounter saying, "You were looking for able-bodied people and overlooked us. But Jesus took us seriously; we haven't looked back since."

■ *Jesus Heals the Leper*

6th Sunday of Ordinary Time (B)   *John 15:9-17*

As Jesus was walking through the towns of Galilee he was

> seeing and feeling,
> touching and healing

the sores, the illnesses, and the suffering of the people. They all marveled and were astonished at this great prophet-healer the Almighty had sent to them. It seemed there wasn't an ailment or a disease that could not be healed by this man. There were, however, waves of whispering voices that kept saying he would not dare set foot in the leper colony. The whispers grew louder and more intense, saying he would not dare touch those

> God-forsaken,
> God-forgotten,
> God-awful people.

Because lepers were the exiled people of that age, anyone ever seen with a leper would be banished themselves because everyone dreaded this contagious disease. People with leprosy often hid themselves from the public because of the shame it brought them. They were indeed a disgusting, nauseating sight to see. Those unfortunate enough to have the illness would have to leave town and seek shelter in caves out in the country-side—away from the inhabitants.

As time went on, Jesus expelled the demon, cured Peter's mother-in-law of a severe fever. He told Jairus his daughter was not dead—just asleep; and a woman, in a leap of faith, touched his garment and was healed of her hemorrhage.

But would he set foot in a leper colony?

Jesus gave sight to the blind, and told the paralytic to take his mat and walk. Jesus got into trouble when healing the man with the shriveled hand in the synagogue on the sabbath; he calmed a raging, roaring storm that had his disciples in a state of panic.

But would he set foot in a leper colony?

Jesus gave hearing to the deaf and gave a voice to those who could not speak. Jesus touched people of every age:

> He cured a boy with rheumatic fever.
> He healed a woman with pneumonia.
> He was there when smallpox became an epidemic.

But would he set foot in a leper colony?

Jesus healed the man with emphysema. He was there when a friend suffered an aneurysm. He held the hand of a person on a kidney dialysis machine. He never left the girl who had claustrophobia. When a young boy got leukemia, Jesus' eyes filled with tears.

But would he set foot in a leper colony?

Jesus didn't forsake those who contracted AIDS. He encouraged those fighting obesity, told the alcoholic he cared, embraced a young teen who experienced an overdose.

Jesus loved all his people. He told a boy who had sickle cell anemia that he had high hopes for him. When polio reached epidemic proportions, Jesus said he would assist the medical people to gain a cure.

But would he set foot in a leper colony?

Jesus touched the arm of a cerebral palsy victim, wept when the bubonic plague followed a terrible war, comforted a woman fighting cancer, waited at the bedside of a person in a comatose state.

Jesus could be heard by the man struggling with heart disease; he befriended a girl who was an an-orexia patient.

But would he set foot in a leper colony?

Then one day while everyone was speculating among themselves, Jesus slipped off by himself and entered the leper colony. Jesus never thought of what he should do; he simply went up to an ailing man and did a very human thing, an act that pleased God: Jesus hugged and kissed the stranger—and called him Brother.

The leprosy left the man, but Jesus gave him strict orders not to tell anyone about this healing. The baffled man looked in Jesus' eyes and asked, "Why?"

Jesus replied, "For years I have been healing and curing. I have shown people how to help one another. Now it is time for people to do
        the curing,
        the healing,
        the loving."

■ *"...Whoever Is Not Against Us Is For Us"*

26th Sunday of Ordinary Time (B)   Mark 9:38-43, 45, 47-48

There was once a fine young pastor, Paul by name, who preached wonderfully to his congregation every Sunday. This splendid man of the cloth preached stories of Jesus. He told magnificent and inspiring stories about the Christ. Preacher Paul was so creative and clever in his chosen field that people came from all over town to hear his stories

> of healing and love,
> of forgiveness and mercy.

No other preacher could ever hope to match preacher Paul either in style, enthusiasm, or insight. Preacher Paul was indeed a gifted and sharing person.

Not only did preacher Paul tell stimulating stories of Jesus, but he also served the needs of people in his town. His talent and wisdom were instrumental in opening a co-op store, a first in his community. This co-op store helped people save their hard-earned money when they did their weekly grocery shopping.

Without batting an eyelash, preacher Paul also fed the many unfortunates who would come to his door; he would assist the elderly, the prisoners at the county jail, the sick in the nearby hospital. Certainly pastor Paul was to many Jesus incarnated; he seemed to be another Christ on earth.

One Sunday, however, a cloud was cast over the entire community. A new person began to tell wonderful stories of Jesus' mercy and forgiveness to the incarcerated at the county jail. Upon seeing her, a few of the regular churchgoers approached and scolded this fine young woman saying, "You are not to do this! You have not been ordained nor commissioned. Stop this very instant!"

After the confrontation, the people went about their business; that is, they went to their church service. Once inside the church, the group approached the pastor, saying, "There's a certain person creating a nuisance in the county jail, telling stories of Jesus' mercy and forgiveness. We told her to stop because they are your concern."

The preacher responded, "I'll see what's going on there." The group calmed down, for they were satisfied that preacher Paul would be able to put an end to it.

A few minutes later an usher on his way to church heard about this certain young person telling spectacular stories of Jesus' healing power to patients in the nearby hospital. Upon hearing this the usher thought, "Who does she think she is?! We hired someone to do this! Only the preacher is to tell spectacular stories of Jesus' healing power. This has to stop immediately!" When the usher reached the church, he approached the pastor and said, "There's a strange person preaching stories of Jesus' healing power to your sick and infirm. I told the person to stop immediately." And with that, the usher took his proper place at the back of the church.

A couple minutes later, one of the church's lay leaders and several staff members noticed the young woman on the church steps, feeding the unfortunates of the community and telling stories of Jesus' great love and compassion. Upon seeing this, the enraged assembly yelled at the stranger,

     "Who are you?

     You don't belong here!

     Get away from here!

     Move!

     Move!

     You're meddling in the work

       of our pastor,

       of our community.

Now get away from here!" The nearly hysterical assembly approached the preacher at the altar, "There's a stranger on your church steps feeding the poor and telling stories of Jesus' love and compassion. We told her to go away. Something ought to be done about this. This stranger is intruding in our business." At once, the preacher stopped the service in the middle of a scripture reading and said he would handle the situation right away. The entire congregation followed him to the icy church steps.

When preacher Paul and his congregation opened the church door, he spotted the young woman assisting people up the slippery church steps. The pastor inquired of the stranger, "Who are you?"

The woman answered, "I have been a member of the congregation for awhile; haven't you ever noticed me?"

The preacher then asked, "What are you doing?"

The young woman answered, "In God's name, I am doing the Lord's work."

The now indignant pastor charged, "This is
        not your mission,
        not your church,
        not your people,
        not your business,
so leave at once so we can continue our service!"

The woman left, and the service resumed where it had halted. The scripture reading continued: "...whoever is not against us is for us."

■ "...But Do Not Follow Their Example."

31st Sunday of Ordinary Time (A)   *Matthew 23:1-12*

Once, there was a poor widow who lived in a great urban center. The woman's husband had died a few years ago, leaving her in financial difficulty. The widow had but a few dollars to her name, but with her spouse's social security check, the widow managed to pay her rent and buy some much-needed food. No matter how desperate the widow was, she nevertheless made her way to church every week, contributing what little she could afford.

Some, however—the church leaders especially—made fun of the widow whenever she arrived at the church for worship, mocking the pennies she'd deposit in the treasury box. The church leaders were always dressed in splendid clothing, wearing the most eloquent robes and tassels money could buy. Their wardrobes took space equal to that of a prince, or even a king. The automobiles the church leaders drove were above average to those seen on the streets; they drove in style and luxury in

their Cadillacs,
their Lincolns, and
their Rolls Royces.

One day as the widow was on her way to church, she saw a shiny silver coin lying on the dirt road she was traveling. After stooping to pick up the unusual coin, the likes the widow had never seen, she put the coin in her purse and continued on her way.

Arriving at the church, the widow solemnly entered the edifice. As she did, the widow noticed a group of robed leaders putting their contributions into the treasury box. Though the leaders' dollars made not a sound, the widow and everyone else heard their loud conversation.

The first leader spoke:

"I am contributing my IBM dividend check to help our church. I bought my stocks many years ago when I was an apprentice in the ministry. The stocks have risen in value ten-, even a hundred-fold. I thought it would be rather selfish of me if I didn't assist the church in its time of need. I will henceforth generously contribute this modest share of my wealth."

The second leader spoke:

"I am gladly contributing my $1200 monthly pension check from the government. I was a chaplain in the Navy for twenty-five years and reached the rank of rear admiral. I helped our sailors through very hard times while at sea far away. When I retired, I received a commission of full admiral for life. With that commission, my pension increased generously—and I want to be just as generous to the church."

The third leader spoke:

"I am contributing my pastoral stipends from the many baptisms, weddings, funerals, and other services that I performed throughout the year. The people have been so kind to me that I feel obliged to contribute. I see great growth for our church if everyone contributes equally. And shame on those who don't contribute; I wonder what comes before church?!"

The fourth leader spoke:

"I am contributing all the honorariums that I have received for my many speaking engagements. I travel across the country, unrelentingly speaking about the Lord's love and God's great power. I have witnessed the esteem of people from all walks of life and feel compelled to share a portion of that esteem with the church and its mission."

After the church leaders finished praising themselves, the widow slowly approached the treasury box. Dropping the silver coin into the box, the woman uttered not a word, nor did she look at any of the leaders who she suspected were watching her. The leaders all watched the widow and nodded patronizingly. Each of the leaders, however, glanced at one another, ridiculing the silver coin placed in the box by the widow. The woman left the church shortly afterward.

As was the custom, the moneys deposited into the treasury box were counted by the church leaders. There were
>many checks and currencies,
>many coins and even some I.O.U.'s,
but there was only one silver coin.

The coin was unusual even to the church leaders, who knew their money. The coin was so unusual that they took the piece to the bank so that experts could evaluate their finding.

The bank was stymied by the coin as well; they sent the coin to their headquarters. Meanwhile the religious leaders looked at one another, thinking the coin had obviously been contributed by one of their own class of
>equal wealth,
>equal prestige,
>equal position,
>equal generosity.

The news was relayed to the church leaders that the silver piece was a two-thousand-year-old coin! The coin's worth was considered priceless.

The widow never knew—nor would she have cared. The widow's God was already *priceless!* And the widow was *priceless* in that priceless God's sight!

■ Jesus Calms the Storm

12th Sunday of Ordinary Time (B)   *Mark 4:35-41*

> "Lord help me, my boat is too small
> and the sea is too big."
> — *An old familiar prayer*

Surely all of us, at times, have been buffeted around like helpless wooden matchsticks in this sea of life. No wonder this prayer is appropriate in describing our feelings when storms invade our peace and security. These storms seem to overwhelm us just when things are finally piecing themselves together.

These storms have no respect for age, gender, or position. We are all left defenseless. The only hope for our lives is Jesus. Jesus calmed many storms in his day, but his footsteps are not visible on the beaches as they once were. Jesus went to his Father, but he told us he would be with us always to calm any storm that may come our way. But Jesus hastened to add, "You must have faith and my hand will rescue you."

What follows are the stories of three people whose encounters with such storms—

> the hurricanes,
> the tornadoes, and
> the squalls of life—

and the willingness of others to lend a hand are worth telling. By their own admission, those who lent the helping hand were people without faith. What they shared and gave to others, however, is a healthy understanding of what Jesus meant by faith. They have names and occupations.

When Larry first met John, a doctor, his boat was shipwrecked and death seemed to be the only way out. The doctor saw two different people within Larry. One was Larry's enemy, bent on destruction, a person unconscious of loving or of being loved, a person riddled with self-pity and lacking self-esteem.

The other person within Larry, the doctor observed, was a person capable of compassion, capable of caring, a person who could persevere against all odds.

The doctor chose to rescue the second person, and in doing so, gave Larry a new life with a rekindled spirit of hope.

The doctor often said that he lacked faith—but what Larry saw was a person of immense faith.

When Steve first met one of his professors, Paul, he was wallowing under the heavy burden of resentment and disdain by his peers. Steve was struggling with the inability of his peers to accept his ministry to God's poor. Steve's "theology of dirty hands" seemed useless and fruitless, and he was convinced his work should not continue.

Steve's ability to stay afloat during the constant torrential downpour of criticism began to wane. He began to sink.

Then a moment came—he felt a hand. Paul, his professor, said to the class of theology students, "If, if you really believe in the faith that you say you have, then go out and do something with it." With that, the professor left the classroom and an eerie silence permeated the room. It was a signal for Steve to continue his ministry of service.

The professor would often say that he lacked faith—but what Steve observed was a man of extraordinary faith.

One memorable encounter with my best friend Michael, a pimp, brought the reality to mind that a strong hand in stormy times may not be visible nor even felt. Sometimes it is one's own secret.

What prompted this encounter was the raging tide of frustration and bewilderment I felt after my failed attempts to secure a summer job while taking care of my ailing mother. Being desperate and greatly exasperated, I sought Michael out for a job, a job at his business establishment doing work he could easily offer me.

As I was sipping my beer and presenting Michael with my appeal, he quickly got up and gave me a curt and emphatic "No." I was left speechless and grasped for some sort of understanding as to why he wouldn't help me. Later that night I went to my friend's home for some answers. The reply Michael gave me was indeed my "saving hand." "I want you to be a priest," he said. "I don't want anything to stand in your way of helping people. I am not going to tempt you with any roadblocks."

In retrospect, Michael's words were an affirmation of my person and ministry. Michael's words also said something good about my friend.

Michael was a person who had given up his faith—but what I sensed was a person who recognized faith.

      The doctor,
      the professor, and
      the pimp

were persons who claimed little or no faith—but look what they accomplished!

■ *The Penitent Woman*

11th Sunday of Ordinary Time (C)   *Luke 7:36-50*

Like most children, I grew attached to a toy given to me as I celebrated an early birthday. I loved my ceramic pony so much that I used to take it to bed with me.

With a streak of white across
        its brown body,
        its dark brown eyes,
        its long wavy tail,
        its muscular frame,
"Sam" shared my room with me and I felt very much protected. I am sure, if my pony could have spoken, it would have expressed similar feelings.

I treasured my pony coming to bed with me.

Getting up in the middle of the night and feeling quite restless, I took my pony to the kitchen to raid the refrigerator of the left-over chicken. As I reached for a chicken leg, my pony slipped from my hand and fell to the floor. Sam's right leg broke in the fall.

Tears flowed from my eyes as I picked up my pony, hoping to restore it to good health. I didn't know what could be done to repair my toy. I knew I wanted something done in a second, right away! But I knew it would take time 'cause things didn't work that way, ever.

The next morning I attempted to repair my pony.

The first thing I thought of was my shoestrings. I untied them from my brand-new shoes, tied them together and wrapped them around my pony's legs up to its stomach. Though it looked a bit sloppy, I was hoping it would do the trick. I stood my pony on my bureau where it generally stood—but it fell.

Thinking of a better idea, I got a bunch of rubber bands, tied them all together as I had done with the shoestrings. I again wrapped this new concoction around the pony's legs and stomach. But again, my pony failed to stand properly and fell.

Moving beyond these failed endeavors, I decided to use some Scotch tape that I found in my drawer. Even that failed to restore my pony to its original state.

I finally used Elmer's glue. "It did the trick," I exclaimed with excitement. I was indeed pleased that my pony was restored. But though it was "fixed," it wasn't exactly the same toy it was before the accident. Bringing my "healed" pony to bed with me was actually an exercise in being overly careful about how to place my toy in my bed. I was very careful not to put Sam in any awkward positions. I was always conscious of my pony's limitations.

Though the glue did a much better job than the shoestrings, rubber bands, and tape, its holding power lasted but a few weeks. You can imagine my disappointment when I saw my pony lying on my bureau with its leg next to it.

We live in a world of immediacy; we want quick solutions to all our problems—and the quicker they come, the better they are.

We live in a world of rapid movement and expectation:

> instant printing;
> fast food,
> automatic cash;
> prompt service;
> spontaneous news;
>> in a jiffy;
>> in a flash;
> *Pronto!*

We live in a world where we don't always have
> time to act,
> just react.

In our gospel story, Jesus healed the sins of a woman
> whose life had come apart,

> whose life was
> broken,
> shattered.

Only in Jesus' actions can immediate and spontaneous love and forgiveness occur. The woman in our scripture story had shown deep remorse and love by her actions, and she was healed on the spot. By the very act of Jesus' love, she was made whole again.

Simon, the Pharisee and detractor, and the others with him, however, were critical of Jesus' acceptance of the woman. They could not believe what they heard and saw in their very presence.

Instead of being critical of Jesus, we accept his invitation to follow him and in doing so, we allow our faith to recognize God's power working through the Master's actions to heal all people.

■ *Blind Man at Jericho*

30th Sunday of Ordinary Time (B)   *Mark 10:46-52*

I am sure many of us can recall the scenes of Pope
John Paul II traveling in his motorcade during his
epic first journey to the United States. The news
magazines, *Time, Newsweek,* and *U.S. News and
World Report,* all praised what they called "the
charismatic leader of our time." Now John Paul is
but one of many charismatic leaders who have
touched us: there were
> Martin and Robert,
> Hubert and Sam,
> Anwar, and the unforgettable
> Mother Teresa rescuing unwanted
> > children in war-torn Lebanon.

But I guess the moment I will never forget was
back in the final days of the 1960 presidential cam-
paign, when John Kennedy was taking a motorcade
ride through downtown Philadelphia. I was one of
500,000 people cheering him. Only fourteen at the
time, what I remember most of all was
> a feeling,
> a feeling of anticipation,

a feeling of hope,
a feeling of a better future
for all because of this man's vision. I wanted to
break through the police barricades to shake his
hand, but the police officers kept screaming, "No!
No! No!" Kennedy's motorcade, however, slowed
down and stopped as if he wanted to touch the
people's hands. Ignoring the police, I broke through
and shook the future president's hand!

In similar fashion we can relate to the gospel reading in which Jesus is entering the downtown area of
Jericho. Jesus is on the move, a motorcade of sorts,
with a crowd of people cramming the roads, following him. Jesus' disciples are protecting him as if
they are secret service agents, while there,
on the other side of the road,
on the sideline
stands a lonely man named Bartimaeus.

Bartimaeus has an impediment: he is blind, and he
feels he needs to see to achieve
that vision,
that promise,
that future Jesus is proclaiming.

Nonetheless Bartimaeus starts shouting, "Son of
David, have pity on me!" The crowd, being irritated,
puts their fingers to their lips and looks directly at
Bartimaeus. They begin "Shhh-ing" him. When
Bartimaeus fails to acknowledge their order, they
begin to admonish him,
"be quiet,
be still,
shut up!"

Bartimaeus persists—and attracts the attention of Jesus. Jesus recognizes the faith of the blind man and responds to his life-long wish:

> to see
> to have vision.

Jesus touches the man's hand and cures Bartimaeus' blindness. Bartimaeus begins following Jesus to live out that vision we continue to call "The Kingdom of God."

Bartimaeus

> doesn't remain on the sideline of life,
> isn't somewhere else when help is
>   needed,
> can't remain silent on the roadside
>   when voices need to be heard.

Bartimaeus is there when human injustice and human suffering need to be healed.

Bartimaeus

> takes the vision,
> takes the message,
> takes the promise

and follows Jesus. Though blind, Bartimaeus has vision, is truly gifted, and responds. Bartimaeus, once given sight,

> takes to the road,
> moves from the sidelines,
> goes to the other side

and gives

> that vision of Jesus,
> that vision of discipleship,
> that vision of the Kingdom

and takes it to the limit.

■ *Casting Out the Unclean Spirit*

4th Sunday of Ordinary Time (B)   *Mark 1:21-28*

"Come out of the man!"
...The unclean spirit...came out of him.

In today's gospel we learn about the unclean spirit. At another time it will be called "The Evil One"; another time, "a demon". Later in scripture the unclean spirit will be personalized with the name "Satan." Whatever its name, the spirit that lived in and controlled the man in our scripture story was a force to be reckoned with.

This spirit lived, in a demonic way, a life that otherwise would probably have been normal. The evil one living in the man repudiated any semblance of goodness in him.

The wretched body somehow survived in hope for the day when someone,

> a doctor,
> a therapist,
> a specialist,

might be able to relieve it of this horrible anomaly.

Then one day the man with the unclean spirit walked across the path of the Messiah. He couldn't hide the sheer hope that this man might alleviate all the intolerable turmoil inside him. The evil spirit knew the Messiah as well—and feared the power of God that dwelled in that extraordinary person.

The unclean spirit, as the Prophet had demanded, left the man only to reside in someone else;
> to control others;
> to dispel the goodness of humanity.

The Evil One is indeed alive
> because of the imperfect world we live in;
> because of the imperfect age we are part of;
> because we ourselves are imperfect, and we see imperfection around us.

The Evil One is indeed a part of our very existence because we can *see* the wrongs of life: *ours* and *others*.

Seldom do we *see* Satan, yet we know he's around.

Satan is around not so much within individuals but in what individuals do to one another. Last week, for example, I *saw* Satan before me often.
> Last Sunday, while watching the Super Bowl game, an alcoholic father was abusive to his wife and children.

On Monday, missiles were fired from jet
bombers, causing death and
destruction in their wake.
On Tuesday, the cover of *Newsweek
Magazine* showed a captured
prisoner-of-war who had been beaten
severely in the face.
On Wednesday, at a detention center
was an eighteen year old arrested for
possession of crack and for plundering
his grandmother's house, seeking
money for his habit.
On Thursday, a police officer was
suspended from the force after
beating a suspect and paralyzing him
for life.
On Friday, an inner-city supermarket
raised the price of a gallon of milk
three times higher than its sister
market in a better part of town.

Satan continued to live by those activities last
week.
Day after day,
week after week,
month after month,
year after year,
decade after decade,
century after century,
Satan continues to live.

But on Saturday, in the lives of a few people, Satan
died.

A young man was welcomed home for Christmas by his parents. His father shared with me that it was "Mike's coming home to die." Mike had gone to work in New York City where he fell ill to a disease. That disease was diagnosed as AIDS.

As with most people who have contracted AIDS, Mike went through the trauma of having people refuse to associate with him. People who should have known better shunned Mike because of their fears. Even church doors were slammed in his face.

Mike, in many ways, felt contaminated.
> He wasn't invited;
> he was rejected.
> He left angry and resentful; but
> he felt compassion

for those unfortunate enough to not understand. Mike knew why people looked at him as they did. Mike also knew that people's vision of him was blurred with only tactics that Satan would use. Life was certainly not easy for the young man.

Though Mike was in touch with his parents, he must have felt a bit uneasy about coming home with a disease that had found so little sympathy elsewhere. Far beyond sympathy, Mike received understanding and love.

It was no wonder that Mike came home to die last Christmastime. He came to a home filled with love and understanding. His was also a family who knew how to meet the Satans of the world—and in this disease, the hearts of Mike's family met Satan face-to-face.

At the hospital, Satan worked as he had for ages to divide a family. But the family didn't give in to the fear, the pain, the helplessness, the sordid views of life, as Satan had hoped and expected them to do. The family continued to grow together in a faith that only produced love.

And when the moment came:
>the disease died;
>the son, with a loving embrace,
>>returned to his Creator;
>the evil one disappeared from the scene.

The family had won!

Their son returned to God as their gift. They won, for they had dared to love. Now, this family is assisting others to win over Satan by truly loving—and letting that love grow and multiply.

For love is everywhere. It is only when love dies that life is given to the evil one.

■ *Peter's Confession*

24th Sunday of Ordinary Time (B)   *Mark 8:27-35*

He was like
>>> some sort of Titan,
>>> some sort of Hercules,
>>> some sort of Superman—
>>>> untarnished,
>>>> unblemished, and
>>>> unruffled

when confronted by those scoundrels, "the know-it-all people" who were affiliated with the Pharisees and the Sadducees. When pitted against some of the scribes and leaders of the Sanhedrin, he knew his stuff—and all were astonished by his greatness. He challenged their power game
>>> of authority,
>>> of law,
>>> of manipulation,
>>> of morality,

and won the admiration of his disciples.

As you can imagine, his disciples were not fond of nor did they admire bright people who were in awe of themselves and who classified themselves as

> clever,
> brilliant, and
> ingenious.

His disciples were plain folks who worked at their trade as their fathers and their fathers' fathers had.

Moreover, his disciples were actually aware of the works of their God. They were keenly aware that Yahweh had placed the eternal imprint on the design and works of

> Samuel,
> Saul, and
> David;
> Jacob and
> Jonah;
> Abraham and
> Moses.

When he called his disciples to follow him, they looked at him somewhat strangely.

> He looked different;
> he acted different;
> he promised different things.

Nevertheless they decided to follow him though they knew not what to expect. Perhaps they were seeking

> adventure,
> excitement, and
> something unusual—certainly not fame
>   and fortune.

The disciples traveled the many miles with him:

He ousted Satan—and they said
   wonderful.
He straightened a withered hand—and
   they said marvelous.
He calmed a storm—and they said
   beautiful.

They saw him
     feed thousands,
     cure thousands,
     forgive thousands—and they said
     tremendous!

And then he put them on the spot: "Who do people say I am?"

"Oh, some say you're Moses, Abraham, Elijah or one of the other prophets. Others say you're the Baptist. Still others say you're the devil in disguise because—"

He interrupted them in mid-sentence, "But who do *you* say I am?"

On the spot again, the disciples, their adrenaline now flowing, abruptly answered, "You're
     our Leader,
     our Liberator!"
Another, "You're
     our avenger,
     our equalizer!"
Still another, "You're
     our hero,
     our freedom fighter,
     our ticket to paradise!"

Peter's voice smothered all other voices when he shouted,"You are the Anointed One of God; you are God's Son!"

And Jesus said, "*I am he.* Yet I will endure humiliation, suffer and give up my life."

Peter, on hearing this, burst into laughter, "Suffer? Die?!
>Have you gone delirious?
>Have you taken leave of your senses?"

And Peter continued,
>"Patriarchs suffer—not heroes!
>Prophets are humiliated—not *you!*
>False gods die—not God's only Son!
>Real gods live—never die!
>Real gods never give in or give up!
>Real gods are always there—so,
>>you mustn't suffer,
>>*you* mustn't die!"

But Jesus responded: "*Peter!*
>This is the way it must be!
>This is the way it must be for *my*
>>mission to be accomplished!"

■ *Comparing the Kingdom*

17th Sunday of Ordinary Time (A)   *Matthew 13:44-52*

"The kingdom of heaven is like a treasure buried
in a field, which a person finds..."

While Jesus and his disciples were relaxing after a
hectic day of traveling and spreading the Good
News, a discussion arose as to what the Kingdom of
God could be compared to. Jesus responded to their
question: "The Kingdom of God can be compared to
a divorced woman with three children who was in
the grip of financial straits when she was informed
she had won the state lottery for ten million dollars!
The Kingdom of God," Jesus continued, "can also be
compared to someone seeing a magnificent rainbow
after a torrential summer rainstorm!"

The disciples, though excited by what they heard,
weren't too sure they really fully understood what
Jesus was explaining to them. As they sat by the
wood fire, playfully anticipating further revelations
as to what the Kingdom of God was all about, Jesus
continued: "The Kingdom of God can be likened to a

housewife who goes to bed knowing there is peace in the home, and the Kingdom of God can be compared to a family sitting at a table of festive food on Thanksgiving Day, offering thanks to one another and to God."

"More!" shouted the disciples.

Agreeably, Jesus began again, "The Kingdom of God can be compared to a relationship gone sour and after several years of much-needed maturation, understanding and trust is shared and love blossoms."

The disciples, now thinking they understood the issue, also wanted to speculate on this question, hoping to get the approval of Jesus.

The first disciple began, "The Kingdom of God can be compared to a high school student who receives an 'A' on an algebra test though she only expected a 'D'!"

"You're on the right track," Jesus said, affirming the disciple's example.

Another disciple, taking his turn, stood up and declared: "The Kingdom of God can be likened to a little boy who sees only one box for him under the Christmas tree and feels disappointed—only to open the box to find the puppy he had yearned to have!"

Jesus nodded his encouragement with a smile.

Another jumped in by saying: "The Kingdom of God can be compared to a woman lost on a remote road at night with the gas gauge pointing to 'empty'— and then she sees the bright neon lights of a service station!"

"Yes, but even more!" Jesus exclaimed, adding, "The Kingdom of God can be compared to a woman who for ten years was told she could not bear a child—but then gives birth to twins!"

At this, a disciple more confident now than when the discussion began, suggested, "The Kingdom of God can be likened to a deaf person who after an operation hears the sounds of the birds chirping for the first time!"

"Pretty good!" smiled the Master.

Another disciple added, "The Kingdom of God can be compared to a house that was the sore spot in a community, but which the community renovated into a structure that served as a place where the neglected could be treated like kings!"

"Very good!" the Teacher commented.

Another disciple spoke, "The Kingdom of God can be likened to a heart-maker who created people only to see them threaten, battle and kill one another. To solve the problem, this person placed a heart into each person that enabled people to share, care and love each other!"

Some of the disciples shrugged their shoulders as if to say "So what?" Others were delighted with the disciple's insight.

But another disciple exclaimed, "That's ridiculous, the silliest thing I ever heard."

Others clamored,
>   "Ludicrous!
>   Absurd!
>   Idiotic!"

Still others,
>   "That's nonsense!
>   It's baloney!
>   Rubbish!"

As the commotion subsided, a disciple questioned the speaker, "What makes you think anyone can change a person just by giving that person a heart? You're not in the real world."

As others continued to comment on this question, Jesus congratulated the disciple who had ventured to use the image of a heart. Some disciples, despite Jesus' words, remained annoyed. Jesus suggested a good night's sleep would help all to understand the Kingdom of God a bit better.

After a long walk, Jesus and the disciples arrived at their house very tired and worn out. Unfortunately however, the disciple whose comment was responsible for the disciples' annoyance had lost the key to the house on the way home.

Tempers exploded in every direction when the exhausted disciples realized they were locked out.

Their clamoring awakened a neighbor from a deep sleep. Peering from his window, he shouted down to the disciples, "What's going on? It's two in the morning!"

In a chorus, the disciples answered, "We're locked out." Seeing that it was beginning to rain and the temperature close to freezing, the neighbor invited the disciples in for the night, saying, "There's plenty of room here for everyone; enough blankets and good food."

As the disciples made themselves at home, Jesus reminded them: "The Kingdom of God is also like a neighbor whose tender heart enabled him to share, care and love enough to open his door to noisy, arguing people at two in the morning!"

Scripture Index

GUIDES FOR STORYTELLERS

Story As a Way to God: A Guide for Storytellers

H. Maxwell Butcher

Paper, $9.95
160 pages, 5½ x 8½
ISBN 0-89390-201-2

Why are stories so powerful? Find out why every good story—from *The Ugly American* to *West Side Story*—says something about the divine. Learn how to find God's story in the Bible and elsewhere. Explore four different ways to tell God's story.

Storytelling Step by Step

Marsh Cassady

Paper, $9.95
168 pages, 5½ x 8½
ISBN 0-89390-183-0

The author takes you through all the steps in telling stories: selecting the right story for your audience, adapting your story for different occasions, analyzing it so that you can present it well, preparing your audience, and, finally, presenting your story. Includes sample stories.

Creating Stories for Storytelling

Marsh Cassady

Paper, $9.95
144 pages, 5½ x 8½
ISBN 0-89390-205-5

This book picks up where *Storytelling Step by Step* leaves off. Find out how to create your own original stories, adapt stories to different audiences, plot a story, create tension, and write dialogue to keep your listeners on the edge of their chairs.

Order from your local bookseller, or use the order form on the last page.

STORIES FOR GROWTH & CHANGE

Breakthrough:
Stories of Conversion

Andre Papineau

Paper, $7.95
144 pages, 5½" x 8½"
ISBN 0-89390-128-8

This resource will help you and your group witness what takes place inside people as they change, reminding you that change, ultimately, is a positive experience. Reflections from a psychological point of view will help you help others through their personal conversions.

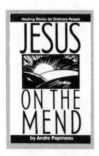

Jesus on the Mend:
Healing Stories for
Ordinary People

Andre Papineau

Paper, $7.95
152 pages, 5½" x 8½"
ISBN 0-89390-140-7

These Gospel-based stories illustrate four aspects of healing: Acknowledging the Need, Reaching Out for Help, The Healer's Credentials, and The Healer's Therapy. Helpful reflections focus on the process of healing that takes place.

Biblical Blues:
Growing Through
Setups and Letdowns

Andre Papineau

Paper, $7.95
160 pages, 5½" x 8½"
ISBN 0-89390-157-1

This book of biblical stories acknowledges how people set themselves up for letdowns, then explains how the setup/letdown cycle promotes personal growth.

Order from your local bookseller, or use the order form on the last page.

GOSPEL COMMENTARIES & REFLECTIONS

Cycling Through the Gospels: Gospel Commentaries for Cycles A, B, & C

Jerome J. Sabatowich

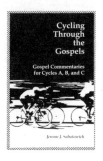

Paper, $19.95
360 pages, 6" x 9"
ISBN 0-89390-207-1

Are you looking for authoritative background on the Sunday Gospels in an easy-to-digest style? The author answers your questions about the readings, covering all three liturgical cycles and major feasts. These commentaries are great for Sunday bulletins, personal reflection, or group study.

Gospel Bites: Illustrated Wisdom for Lectionary Cycles A, B, & C

Joseph Noonan
Joseph Nolan

Paper, $10.95
200 pages, 4" x 7"
ISBN 0-89390-239-X

What happens when biblical values collide with modern realities? You get a Joseph Noonan cartoon. Biblical and contemporary characters whine, snarl, probe, and change the subject—all in response to the Gospel. They struggle to fit their diets, their Mercedes payments, and their kids' college educations into what they heard on Sunday. They poke at Jesus and he pokes back. The gospel never seemed more alive. One cartoon for each Sunday of the three-year lectionary cycle—plus a short meditation from Father Joseph Nolan. Ideal for parish bulletins and newsletters.

Order from your local bookseller, or use the order form on the last page.

STORIES FOR FAITH-SHARING

Stories for
Christian Initiation

Joseph J. Juknialis

Paper, $8.95
160 pages, 5½" x 8½"
ISBN 0-89390-235-7

These stories are organized around the adult catechumenate. These imaginative tales resonate with key lectionary passages and stages of the catechumenate. Each story includes reflections, questions, and ritual.

Stories to Invite
Faith-Sharing:
Experiencing the Lord
through the Seasons

Mary McEntee McGill

Paper, $8.95
128 pages, 5½" x 8½"
ISBN 0-89390-230-6

Read these stories by yourself or with a group. Each season includes five stories and Reflection and Faith-Sharing sections to experience each story and season more fully.

The Light in the Lantern:
True Stories for Your
Faith Journey

James L. Henderschedt

Paper, $8.95
158 pages, 5½" x 8½"
ISBN 0-89390-209-8

Use these stories for personal reflection, homily preparation, or small-group work.

Order from your local bookseller, or use the order form on the last page.

IDEAS FOR PREACHING & TEACHING

Seasonal Illustrations for Preaching and Teaching

Donald L. Deffner

Paper, $11.95
144 pages, 5½" x 8½"
ISBN 0-89390-234-9

"Jesus told stories. Why don't we?" asks the author. Preachers and teachers: use this book of sermon illustrations to get the attention of your listeners and enrich their understanding of the Sunday readings. Includes "Criteria for the Use of Illustrations."

Sermons for Sermon Haters

Andre Papineau

Paper, $10.95
184 pages, 5½" x 8½"
ISBN 0-89390-229-2

In his new book, *Sermons for Sermon Haters,* Andre Papineau shows you how to break open the Gospel in ways that reach even the most jaded.

The Mighty Mustard Bush

Kenneth Guentert

Paper, $8.95
144 pages, 5½" x 8½"
ISBN 0-89390-184-9

Whether you need inspiration for a homily or a new outlook on a season, break out your copy of *The Mighty Mustard Bush* and read just one chapter. The author's biblical sensibility, combined with his down-to-earth wit, will get you going every time.

Order from your local bookseller, or use the order form on the last page.

MORE STORIES FROM LOU RUOFF

For Give: Stories of Reconciliation

Lou Ruoff

Paper, $8.95
120 pages, 5 ½" x 8 ½"
ISBN 0-89390-198-9

The author combines stories from the Bible with his own experiences. In the power and simplicity of his stories, he draws the reader to trust in God's love to forgive and be forgiven.

No Kidding, God, Where Are You? Parables of Ordinary Experience

Lou Ruoff

Paper, $7.95
120 pages, 5 ½" x 8 ½"
ISBN 0-89390-141-5

Lou Ruoff, with his keen perception of the average person's pain, uses his wonderful storytelling gifts to apply the lessons in Jesus' parables to the commonplace happenings of modern life.